PRISONER FOR LIBERTY

by Marty Rhodes Figley

illustrations by Craig Orback

On My Own

HISTORY

M Millbrook Press/Minneapolis

To Candice,
a treasured friend —M.R.F.

For Kelly Wilmeth,
a true friend and supporter —C.S.O.

The illustrator would like to thank Mychal Harris, who modeled for the character James Forten, James Gregor as Henry Bazely, Evan Pengra Sult as Daniel Brewton, and Ramona Harris as James's mother.

Millbrook Press
A division of Lerner Publishing Group, Inc.
241 First Avenue North
Minneapolis, MN 55401 USA

For reading levels and more information, look up this title at www.lernerbooks.com.

Library of Congress Cataloging-in-Publication Data

Figley, Marty Rhodes, 1948–
    Prisoner for liberty / by Marty Rhodes Figley ; illustrations by Craig Orback.
        p.   cm. —   (On my own history)
    Includes bibliographical references and index.
    ISBN 978–0–8225–7280–0 (lib. bdg. : alk. paper)
    ISBN 978–0–7613–4022–5 (EB pdf)
    1. Forten, James, 1766–1842—Childhood and youth—Juvenile literature. 2. African Americans—Biography—Juvenile literature. 3. African American boys—Biography—Juvenile literature. 4. African American soldiers—Biography—Juvenile literature. 5. Prisoners of war—United States—Biography—Juvenile literature. 6. Philadelphia (Pa.)—History—Revolution, 1775–1783—African Americans—Juvenile literature. 7. United States—History—Revolution, 1775–1783—African Americans—Juvenile literature. 8. Free African Americans—Pennsylvania—Philadelphia—Biography—Juvenile literature. 9. Sailmakers—Pennsylvania—Philadelphia—Biography—Juvenile literature. 10. Philadelphia (Pa.)—Biography—Juvenile literature. I. Orback, Craig, ill. II. Title.
E185.97.F717F54 2008
973.3'71092—dc22 [B]   2006028582

Manufactured in the United States of America
4-44251-8116-5/23/2017

Author's Note

James Forten was born on September 2, 1766, in Philadelphia, Pennsylvania. His parents were free African Americans. His grandparents had been slaves. They may have bought their freedom. Or they may have been set free.

James's father was a sailmaker. As a young boy, James went to work with his father and began to learn how to make sails. When James was seven years old, his father died. For a few years, James went to a Quaker school. He learned to read and work with numbers. But his family needed money. So James took a job in a store. James gave the money he earned to his family.

Philadelphia was the largest city in the American colonies. Great Britain ruled the colonies. By the 1770s, the colonists wanted their freedom. In 1776, the leaders of the American colonies signed the Declaration of Independence. James joined the crowd in Philadelphia to hear the Declaration read to the public for the first time. America would still have to fight Great Britain to become free. James wanted to do his part in the fight.

October 8, 1781

James Forten carried gunpowder to
the cannons of the *Royal Louis*.
The powder boy was fifteen years old.
James was proud to fight in the war.
He wanted to help America win freedom
from Great Britain.
The wind blew hard,
and the seas were rough.
James knew he must pay attention
to his job.
If he stumbled,
the gunpowder could explode.
His ship was being chased.
The *Royal Louis* was trying to outrun
the British warship *Amphion*.

The *Amphion* was a bigger ship
with more cannons.
The *Amphion* chased the *Royal Louis*
all morning and into the afternoon.
After seven hours, it was caught.

The *Royal Louis*'s brave captain gave up.
He ordered that the American flag
be lowered.
James was taken to the *Amphion*
with some of the *Royal Louis*'s crew

Angry gray waves
tossed the small boat.
It moved closer to the enemy ship.
James closed his hand over
the bag of marbles in his pocket.
He always carried them for good luck.
But he didn't feel lucky now.
James was one of 20 black sailors
on the *Royal Louis*.

Were the others worried too?
The British and Americans traded
white prisoners of war.
But black prisoners were not usually
traded for other prisoners.
They were often sold into slavery.
James wondered if he would ever
return home again.
He wondered if he would
end up a slave.

October 9, 1781

James woke up cold and stiff.
The prisoners had spent the night
crowded into the cargo space
of the *Amphion*.
In the morning, they were herded up
to the ship's main deck.
James grabbed his sailor's bag.
It held his Bible, hammock,
and clothes.
Captain Bazely and the crew of
the *Amphion* stood waiting for them.
Some of the prisoners from the *Royal
Louis* were sent to another ship.
James was sad to see them go.

He searched his pocket
for his favorite marble.
It felt cool and smooth in his hand.
He watched Captain Bazely talk
to a blond-haired boy.

They stared at James.
James tried to stand tall
and look the captain in the eye.
His mother had taught him to never
bow his head before another man.

The captain and the boy walked over.

"What's your name, lad?"

asked the captain.

"James Forten, sir."

"What's that you have in your hand?"

asked the boy.

James said, "It's my lucky blue marble."

The boy smiled.

"My name is Henry Bazely.

Do you have any more marbles?"

James nodded.

He showed Henry his marble bag.

"Would you fancy a game?"

asked Henry.

James looked at Captain Bazely.

The captain nodded,

then walked away.

James divided his marbles.

He gave some to Henry.

"Were you a slave in America before
you became a sailor?" asked Henry.

"No, I was born free." James said.

"America is as much my country
as it is any man's."

Henry muttered, "Now you are
a prisoner."
James said, "For my country."
At that moment, he made a decision.
He had been a champion
marble player at home.
Even though he was a prisoner,
he wouldn't let the captain's son win.

James knuckled down
and aimed his shooter marble.
Crack! Crack! Crack!

18

One by one, he knocked

Henry's marbles out of the ring.

Henry shook his head.

"Excellent game!"

He called to Captain Bazely,

"Father, come watch James play.

He's quite amazing!"

They played again,

while the captain watched.

James won the game with ease.

"Well done, lad,"

said Captain Bazely.

He frowned at Henry.

"I expect this young man and

his marbles will keep you busy."

Henry smiled at James.

"This is my first voyage," he said.

"I signed on as my father's servant.

There's not much to do."

James and Henry became friends.

They spent hours exploring the ship.

James knew this freedom
would not last.
The *Amphion* was sailing toward
New York harbor.
There, the prisoners would be
taken to the prison ship *Jersey*.

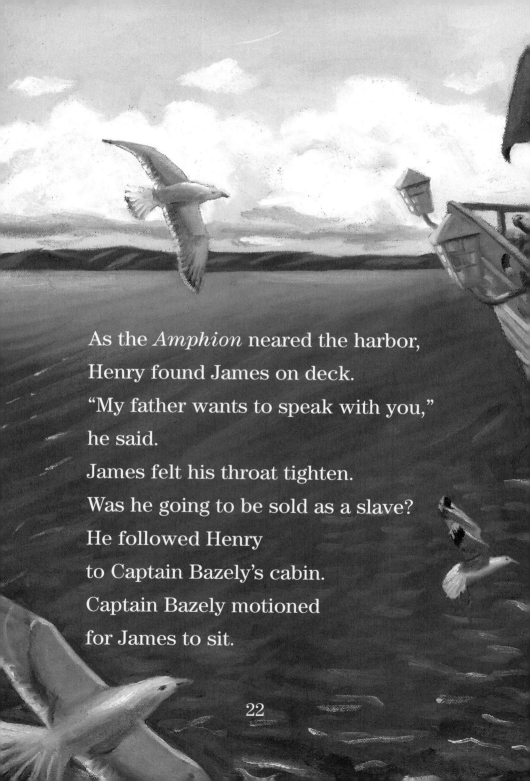

As the *Amphion* neared the harbor,
Henry found James on deck.
"My father wants to speak with you,"
he said.
James felt his throat tighten.
Was he going to be sold as a slave?
He followed Henry
to Captain Bazely's cabin.
Captain Bazely motioned
for James to sit.

22

"James," he said, "Henry and I
are quite impressed by you.
You are brave, independent, and firm.
You are polite and kind."
James said, "Thank you, sir."
Captain Bazely smiled.
"I want to send you to Britain
with my son Henry.
We can do much for you.
You will become a wealthy
and educated man."
Henry said, "Please, James.
Come to Britain with me!"
James stared at his feet.
He remembered July 8, 1776.
All of Philadelphia's bells had rung
in celebration.

A crowd had gathered
around the State House.
Nine-year-old James had pushed
his way to the front.
There he heard the Declaration
of Independence read.
It said that all Americans had
the right to be free.

James knew that many
black Americans were slaves.
He believed in fighting for America's
freedom from Great Britain.
After the war, he wanted to fight for
the right of all black people to be free.

James stood up.

He looked steadily at the captain.

"I have been taken prisoner
for the liberties of my country.
I will never prove a traitor to her,"
he said.

Captain Bazely sighed.

"I understand.
As your friend, I will write a letter
to the prison commander on the *Jersey*.
I will ask him not to forget you
when prisoners are traded."

James thanked Captain Bazely.

As he turned to leave,
he saw Henry's eyes fill with tears.

October 23, 1781

The guard sneered.
"There, Rebels,
there is the cage for you!"
James gasped as they neared
the floating prison.
The *Jersey* had once been
a handsome working ship.
Now it was stripped of guns and sails.
The portholes were sealed shut.
Aboard the *Jersey*,
the air smelled rotten.
It was so thick, James could taste it.
The groans of sick and dying men
filled his ears.

James wondered if he would
leave the ship alive.
He thought of his great-grandfather.
He had been taken from his home
in Africa.
He had sailed to America
on a crowded, dirty slave ship.

How he must have suffered.
But his great-grandfather
had survived.
James vowed that
he would survive too.
One day,
he would return to Philadelphia.

January 1782

James handed Daniel Brewton
a piece of bread.
He watched as the younger boy
tried to chew.
Daniel's red hair was stringy.
His pale skin was slick with sweat.
"Thank you, my friend,"
Daniel whispered.
Daniel was two years younger
than James.
He was already a prisoner on
the *Jersey* when James arrived.

James volunteered for work
on the upper deck.
The air was fresher.
And the guards gave him more food.

The bread was moldy.

The meat was filled with worms.

But the food helped him stay strong.

The ship was an awful place to live.

Men died every day.

Each prisoner waited

for his name to reach the top of a list.

Then he would be traded

for a British prisoner.

Escaping was almost impossible.

When a prisoner tried to swim

to shore, he was caught.

But James was clever.

He discovered how he could leave

the *Jersey.*

An American officer was being traded

for a British officer.

The American officer agreed to let

James hide in his large sea chest.

James visited Daniel one last time.

He gave him an apple that one

of the officers left on deck.

Daniel tried to raise up.

Then he fell back

on his filthy blanket.

"You are so good to me, James."

James tried to ignore the sores

that covered Daniel's face.

He pretended not to hear

the harsh cough that shook

his friend's thin body.

Daniel was getting sicker each day.

He was too weak to climb

to the upper deck.

James knew Daniel couldn't stay

on the *Jersey* much longer.

He would die.

James thought of his mother
and his great-grandfather.
He knew what they would tell him
to do.
James tried to sound cheerful.
"Daniel, you are leaving today,"
he said.
"I've found a way for you to escape!"

Later that evening,
James watched as the officer left.
No one guessed that Daniel was
in the sea chest.
James silently said good-bye
to his friend.

April 1782

James was tired and thin.

But his heart was filled with joy.

Just put one foot in front of the other,

he told himself.

James had spent seven long months

on the prison ship *Jersey*.

The United States had won the war.

James had finally been released.

He knew he had served

his country well.

Tears filled his eyes.

James opened the door.

His mother ran toward him.

"Why, James, you've returned!"

He gave her a hug.

"Yes," he said, smiling. "I'm home."

Afterword

While held prisoner on the *Amphion*, James Forten did become friends with Captain Bazely and his son, Henry. James turned down their offer to go to Great Britain. After he left the *Amphion*, he never saw them again. James later spoke about his experience: "Thus . . . did a game of marbles save [me] from a life of West Indian servitude."

Daniel Brewton never forgot James Forten's kindness. James had given Daniel his chance to escape from the prison ship *Jersey*. Daniel knew that James had saved his life. The two men became lifelong friends.

After the war, James Forten eventually returned to the sailmaking shop where his father had worked. By the age of 32, James owned the shop. He employed 40 men, both white and black. He became one of the wealthiest men in Philadelphia.

James believed that all black Americans were entitled to the same rights enjoyed by white citizens. He was active in the antislavery movement. He helped fund the famous abolitionist newspaper the *Liberator*.

James Forten died on March 4, 1842. More than 3,000 people, both black and white, attended his funeral.

Bibliography

Dring, Thomas. *Recollections of the Jersey Prison-Ship: Taken and Prepared for Publication from the Original Manuscript of the Late Captain Thomas Dring, of Providence, R.I., One of the Prisoners, by Albert G. Green.* Providence: H. H. Brown, 1829; rpt., New York: Corinth Books, 1961.

Gloucester, Stephen H. *A Discourse Delivered on the Occasion of the Death of Mr. James Forten, Sr., in the Second Presbyterian Church of Colour of the City of Philadelphia, April 17, 1842, Before the Young Men of the Bible Association of Said Church.* Philadelphia: I. Ashmead, 1843.

Nell, William C. *The Colored Patriots of the American Revolution.* Boston, 1855; rpt., New York: Arno Press, 1968.

Opie, Iona, and Peter Opie. *Children's Games with Things.* New York: Oxford University Press, 1997.

Purvis, Robert. *Remarks on the Life and Character of James Forten, Delivered at Bethel Church, March 30, 1842.* Philadelphia: Merrihew and Thompson, 1842.

Winch, Julie. *A Gentleman of Color: The Life of James Forten.* New York: Oxford University Press, 2002.